Witness

PATRICK LANE

Witness

Selected Poems 1962–2010

Harbour Publishing

1 2 3 4 5 — 14 13 12 11 10

Harbour Publishing Co. Ltd.
P.O. Box 219, Madeira Park, BC, V0N 2H0
www.harbourpublishing.com

Artwork "October – Barn Owl" by W. Allan Hancock
Poems selected by Patrick Lane with thanks to Silas White
Cover and page design by Anna Comfort
Printed and bound in Canada

Harbour Publishing acknowledges financial support from the Government of Canada through the Canada Book Fund and the Canada Council for the Arts, and from the Province of British Columbia through the BC Arts Council and the Book Publishing Tax Credit.

Library and Archives Canada Cataloguing in Publication

Lane, Patrick, 1939-
     Witness : selected poems 1962-2010 / Patrick Lane.

ISBN 978-1-55017-508-0

     I. Title.

\PS8523.A53A6 2010   C811'.54   C2010-904246-8

This book is for Lorna.

"See how she leans inside the dawn,
the cherry blossoms on her shoulders
as she touches the cat
who follows her everywhere, wanting
only to be with her
among the dark mosses."

from "Stars"
Too Spare, Too Fierce

CONTENTS

FOR TEN YEARS

Tonight the moon slants cold into the snow.
Ice shudders on the glass and suddenly alone
I'm aware of windows. Was it you who told me
you were gone? Beyond the snow
light rides thin as a broken bow
without a hand to guide it. From this hour
darkness comes shrill as a dying bird.

One night in the north you lay in my arms
and wept for a crying bird. In the morning
you found him dead on the window sill.
His beak was a crust of ice
that melted as you breathed.
When I threw him away, he didn't fly.
That country of snow we lived in
was a cushion for owls to walk on.
Birds don't understand windows.
They never did.

SIMILKAMEEN DEER

Driving through the Similkameen valley
I watch for deer on the road.
Miles roll out beneath me. A telegraph key.
A perpetual line of dots.
                              Men here
have put up signs telling me to watch
for rolling rock under the escarpment
of mountains where they've cut stones
for their convenience.

Soon it will be spring and mountains
will lose their somnolence. Snow will melt
and out of a fading
whiteness of mountain cold
there will be deer somewhere
who will have no time to spend
watching for me.

LAST NIGHT IN DARKNESS

Last night in darkness someone killed our cat.
Dipped her in gas. Set her aflame.
Her scattered kittens adorned the yard
in opaque sacks where she aborted them;
none of them burned in her pain.

As I gathered them in a paper bag
I had to pull off slugs
who'd gathered for the feast.
Their scavenger trails hovered
on her body like a mist.

Just to forget her
I leaned heavy in the morning
thrusting with my shovel
deep into earth behind the daisies
reminded only of the other
graves I'd dug

while my son prepared them
for peace. Took each one
out of their paper coffin.
Drove apple blossoms into their eyes –
even the mother who was so scarred.

WILD HORSES

Just to come once alone
to these wild horses
driving out of the high Rockies
raw legs heaving the hip-high snow.

Just once alone. Never to see
the men and their trucks.
Just once alone. Nothing moves
as the stallion with five free mares
rush into the guns. All dead.
Their eyes glaze with frost.
Ice bleeds in their nostrils
as the cable hauls them in.

Later, after the swearing
and the stamping of feet
we ride down into Golden:

Quit bitchin.
It's a hard bloody life
and a long week
for three hundred bucks of meat.

That and the dull dead eyes
and the empty meadows.

BECAUSE I NEVER LEARNED

For my brother John

Because I never learned how
to be gentle and the country
I lived in was hard with dead
animals and men, I didn't question
my father when he told me
to step on the kitten's head
after the bus had run over
its hind quarters.

Now, twenty years later,
I remember only:
the silence of the dying
when the fragile skull collapsed
under my hard bare heel,
the curved tongue in the dust
that would never cry again
and the small of my father's back
as he walked tall away.

ELEPHANTS

The cracked cedar
bunkhouse hangs behind me like a grey pueblo
in the sundown where I sit
to carve an elephant
from a hunk of brown soap
for the Indian boy
who lives in the village a mile back
in the bush.

The alcoholic truck driver
and the cat-skinner sit beside
me with their eyes closed –
all of us waiting out the last hour
until we go back on the grade –

and I try to forget the forever
clank   clank   clank
across the grade
pounding stones and earth to powder
for hours in mosquito-darkness
of the endless cold mountain night.

The elephant takes form –
my knife caresses smooth soap
scaling off curls of brown
which the boy saves to take home
to his mother in the village.

Finished, I hand the carving to him
and he looks at the image of the great
beast for a long time
then sets it on dry cedar
and looks up at me:
                    What's an elephant?

he asks me
so I tell him of the elephants
and their jungles – the story
of the elephant graveyard
which no one has ever found
and how the silent
animals of the rainforest
go away to die somewhere
in the limberlost of distances
and he smiles at me

tells me of his father's
graveyard where his people have been
buried for years. So far back
no one remembers when it started
and I ask him where the graveyard is
and he tells me it is gone
now where no one will ever find it
buried under the grade of the new
highway.

THE BIRD

The bird you captured is dead.
I told you it would die
but you would not learn
from my telling. You wanted
to cage a bird in your hands
and learn to fly.

Listen again.
You must not handle birds.
They cannot fly through your fingers.
You are not a nest
and a feather is
not made of blood and bone.

Only words
can fly for you like birds
on the wall of the sun.
A bird is a poem
that talks of the end of cages.

MOUNTAIN OYSTERS

Kneeling in the sheep shit
he picked up the biggest of the new rams,
brushed the tail aside,
slit the bag,
tucked the knackers in his mouth
and clipped the cords off clean –

the ram   stiff
with a single wild scream

as the tar went on
and he spit the balls in a bowl.

That's how we used to do it
when I was a boy.
It's no more gawdam painful
than any other way
and you can't have rams fightin,
slammin it up every nanny...

and enjoyed them with him,
cutting delicately
into the deep-fried testicles.

Mountain oysters make you strong

he said
while out in the field
the rams stood holding their pain,
legs fluttering like blue hands
of old tired men.

PASSING INTO STORM

Know him for a white man.
He walks sideways into wind
allowing the left of him

to forget what the right
knows as cold. His ears
turn into death what

his eyes can't see. All day
he walks away from the sun
passing into storm. Do not

mistake him for the howl you hear
or the track you think you
follow. Finding a white man

in snow is to look for the dead.
He has been burned by the wind.
He has left too much

flesh on winter's white metal
to leave his colour as a sign.
Cold white. Cold flesh. He leans

into wind sideways; kills without
mercy anything to the left of him
coming like madness in the snow.

THE MAN

Drinking bad whiskey in a bar
on the baked coast of a desert
where the wind never stops moving
and the sand never stops moving
and the sweat never stops moving
down his arms, he wonders
what he is doing beside this woman
whose language he can't speak
and whose body he doesn't know
any better than he knows himself.

He doesn't remember where
he met her or why he is still
with her. He has been watching
two vultures fight over the body
of a rat and he has made a bet
with the fat man who owns the bar
that the bird with one leg will win.

It is the last of his money.
He knows she will leave him
if he loses and he is wondering
what he will do with her if he wins.

AT THE EDGE OF THE JUNGLE

At the edge of the jungle
I watch a dog bury his head
in the mud of the Amazon
to drive away the hovering
mass of flies around his eyes.
The swarm expands like a lung
and settles again on the wound.
Maggots fall away in yellow tears.

I turn to where sunflowers gape
like the vulvas of hanged women.
Everything here is a madness:
a broken melon bleeds a pestilence
of bees; a woman squats and pees
balancing perfectly her basket
of meat; a gelding falls to its knees
under the goad of its driver.

Images catch at my skull like thorns.
I no longer believe
the sight I have been given
and live inside the eyes of a rooster
who walks around a pile of broken bones.
Children have cut away his beak
and with a string have staked him
where he sees but cannot eat.

Diseased clouds bloom in the sky
like black flowers. Heavy with rain
they throw down roots of fire.
The bird drags sound from its skin.
I am grown older than I imagined:
the garden I dreamed does not exist
and compassion is only the beginning
of suffering. Everything deceives.

A man could walk into this jungle
and lying down be lost
among the green sucking of trees.
What reality there is resides
in the child who holds the string
and does not see
the bird as it beats its blunt head
again and again into the earth.

STIGMATA

For Irving Layton

What if there wasn't a metaphor
and the bodies were only bodies
bones pushed out in awkward fingers?
Waves come to the seawall, fall away,
children bounce mouths against the stones
man has carved to keep the sea at bay
and women walk with empty wombs
proclaiming freedom to the night.
Through barroom windows rotten with light
eyes of men open and close like fists.

I bend beside a tidal pool and take a crab from the sea.
His small green life twists helpless in my hand
the living bars of bone and flesh
a cage made by the animal I am.
This thing, the beat, the beat of life
now captured in the darkness of my flesh
struggling with claws as if it could tear its way
through my body back to the sea.
What do I know of the inexorable beauty,
the unrelenting turning of the wheel I am inside me?
Stigmata. I hold a web of blood.

I dream of the scrimshawed teeth of endless whales,
the oceans it took to carve them. Drifting ships
echo in fog the wounds of Leviathan
great grey voices giving cadence to their loss.
The men are gone
who scratched upon white bones their destiny.
Who will speak of the albatross in the shroud of the man,
the sailor who sinks forever in the Mindanao Deep?
I open my hand. The life leaps out.

ALBINO PHEASANTS

At the bottom of the field
where thistles throw their seeds
and poplars grow from cotton into trees
in a single season I stand among the weeds.
Fence posts hold each other up with sagging wire.
Here no man walks except in wasted time.
Men circle me with cattle, cars and wheat.
Machines rot on my margins.
They say the land is wasted when its wild
and offer plows and apple trees to tame
but in the fall when I have driven them away
with their guns and dogs and dreams
I walk alone. While those who'd kill
lie sleeping in soft beds
huddled against the bodies of their wives
I go with speargrass and hooked burrs
and wait upon the ice alone.

Delicate across the mesh of snow
I watch the pale birds come
with beaks the colour of discarded flesh.
White, their feathers are white,
as if they had been born in caves
and only now have risen to the earth
to watch with pink and darting eyes
the slowly moving shadows of the moon.
There is no way to tell men what we do.
The dance they make in sleep
withholds its meaning from their dreams.
That which has been nursed in bone
rests easy upon frozen stone
and what is wild is lost behind closed eyes:
albino birds, pale sisters, succubi.

THE WITNESSES

To know as the word is known, to know little
or less than little, nothing, to contemplate
the setting sun and sit for hours, the world
turning you into the sun as day begins again

To remember words, to remember nothing
but words and make out of nothing the past,
to remember my father, the Macleod Kid
carrying the beat, riding against time

On the rodeo circuit of fifty years ago
the prairie, stretched wet hide
scraped by a knife, disappearing everywhere
to know the Macleod Kid was defeated

To know these things
to climb into the confusions
which are only words, to climb into desire
to ride in the sun, to ride against time

The Macleod Kid raking his spurs on the mare
the cheers from the wagon-backs
where the people sit to watch the local
boy ride against the riders from Calgary

To spit melon seeds into the dust
to roll cigarettes, to leave them hanging
from the lip, to tip your hat back and grin
to laugh or not laugh, to climb into darkness

Below the stands and touch Erla's breast
to eat corn or melons, to roll cigarettes
to drink beer, bottles hidden in paper bags
to grin at the RCMP, horseless, dust on their boots

To watch or not watch, to surround the spectacle
horses asleep in their harness, tails switching
bees swarming on melon rinds, flys buzzing
and what if my words are their voices

What if I try to capture an ecstasy that is not
mine, what if these are only words saying
this was or this was not, a story told to me
until I now no longer believe it was told to me

The witnesses dead? What if I create a past
that never was, make out of nothing
a history of my people whether in pain
or ecstasy, my father riding in the Fort Macleod Rodeo

The hours before dawn when in the last of darkness
I make out of nothing a man riding against time
and thus my agony, the mare twisted sideways
muscles bunched in knots beneath her hide

Her mane, black hair feathered in the wind
that I believe I see, caked mud in her eyes
the breath broken from her body and the Macleod Kid
in the air, falling, the clock stopped?

A MURDER OF CROWS

It is night and somewhere
a tree has fallen across the lines.
There was a time when I would have slept
at the end of the sun and risen with light.
My body knows what I betray.
Even the candle fails, its guttering stub
spitting out the flame. I have struggled
tonight with the poem as never before
wanting to tell you what I know –
what can be said? Words are dark rainbows
without roots, a murder of crows,
a memory of music reduced to guile.
Innocence, old nightmare, drags behind
me like a shadow and today I killed again.

The body hanging down from its tripod.
My knife slid up and steaming ribbons of gut
fell to the ground. I broke the legs
and cut the anus out, stripped off the skin
and chopped the head away; maggots of fat
clinging to the pale red flesh. The death?

If I could tell you the silence
when the body refused to fall
until it seemed the ground reached up
and pulled it down, then I could tell you
everything: what the grass said
to the crows as they passed over,
the eyes of moss, the histories of stone.

It is night and somewhere
a tree has fallen across the lines.
Everything I love has gone to sleep.
What can be said?
The flesh consumes while in the trees
black birds perch waiting first light.
It is night and mountains
and I cannot tell you what the grass said
to the crows as they passed over
can only say how when I looked
I lost their bodies in the sun.

THE MEASURE

For P.K. Page

What is the measure then, the magpie in the field
watching over death, the dog's eyes hard as marbles
breath still frozen to his lips? This quiet repose,

the land having given up the battle against sleep,
the voices crying out beneath the snow.
It is the cold spear of the wind piercing me

that makes me sing of this, the hunger in your eyes.
It is the room of your retreat,
the strain in the hand when it reaches out to touch

the dried and frozen flowers brittle in their vase,
the strain when the mind desires praise...
the music as of soldiers wandering among their dead

or the poor dreaming of wandering as they break
their mouths open to sing as prisoners sing.
Or soldiers marching toward their devotions

or the poor marching or the rich in their dark
rooms of commerce saying this is finally the answer,
this will allow us the right to be and be. To be

anything. In the field the rare
stalks of grass stick stiffly into air.
The poor, the broken people, the endless suffering

we are heir to, given to desire and gaining little.
To fold the arms across the breast and fly
into ourselves. That painless darkness or stand

in the field with nothing everywhere and watch
the first flakes falling and pray for the deliverance
of the grass, a dog's death in the snow? Look

there. Stark as charred bone
a magpie stuns his tongue against the wind
and the wind steals the rattle of his cry.

THE GARDEN

praise the idea
the disordered care
so the stone

you have placed
for beauty continues
with a studied delight

as if a god
had dropped it.
arrange, arrange

plant within
the casual border
your desire.

this is the web
and the ritual of
the web.

what discipline obtains
what way shall you stand
so your eye observes

nothing? the sand
raked into a sea
and the sea

an illusion of sand.
this garden, sprung
from a desire

for order, remains
a scream. it wants
you to want the

storm. it prepares
for rage, the sudden
irrevocable flood.

CHINOOK

Beneath the tree, glutted on winter
apples, seven sparrows lie
drunk, beating small wings on snow
as if they could fly into it
and make of ice an element as free as air.

JUST LIVING

It isn't just violence I told them
in the warm white room below the prairie snow.
It's just another story I no longer know
the truth of, tell it now to hide the holes
when conversation dies. The stories
are like fossils locked in Tyndall stone,
just there and no one knows the meaning.

We were five hours over mountain roads,
the tourniquet wet red and him in the seat
lifting the stump of his arm each mile
looking by the glow of the dash-board lights.
Jesus, he kept saying between cigarettes.
In the pink ice-cream bucket between us
the severed hand sloshed in the melting ice.
He never looked at that.
And then the usual madness, the nurse
wanting his name and birthdate, demanding
his wallet's proof until I lifted his sleeve
and showed her. He grinned at that.
The sight of those veins and tendons
made her turn away. The doctors got him then.
I asked one if he could use the hand
but he said it was probably dead. Too many hours
and, anyway, they couldn't put it back.

On the night-road north
I thought of the saw and the flesh still
hanging from the teeth. They didn't wash it off,
just let it cook in the cants coming down
off the headrig. But that hand in the bucket.
The ice had melted. I emptied the water out,
looked at it curled like an empty cup,
a dark blue spider sleeping. Strange
how the sight of it didn't matter much.
I thought of drying it out and giving it
to him when he got back. I laughed at that,
could see it hanging in the sun

outside his window at the shack.
The light dancing on the nails,
maybe using it for a bird-feeder,
whiskey-jacks perched on the fingers
eating suet from the palm.
I thought those things.
When you're pushing your life
down a tunnel of light
it goes like that. Night and mountains.

I stopped at Mad River bridge.
I'd been driving then eight hours.
But here's the strange part.
I took it out of the bucket and held it
there in the night. It was just meat
you understand. It could have been
a club or a tool for scraping earth,
like when your arm has gone to sleep
and feeling it you know
there's nothing there. What do you do
with the pieces of yourself you lose?
I knew I couldn't keep it and I couldn't
give it to his wife. Bury it?
What for? The life was gone
and he was still alive.
It was cold and it was night and I
had shift-work in the morning.
I threw it high off the bridge
and for one moment it held the moon
still in its fingers before it dropped
into that darkness down below.

THE GREAT WALL

There is a moment on the wall when a man looks out
over the far horizon and wonders when
they will come. He does not know who they are.
The wall was built many years ago, long
before he was born and before his father was
born. All his life has been spent
repairing the wall, replacing the fallen
stones, clearing away the tough grass
that grows like fingers in the masonry.

Inside the wall the land is the same
as outside and once, when he was confused
by the hot wind, he could not remember
which side of the wall he lived on and he
has never forgotten the doubt of that day.
He has seen no one but his family for years.
They were given this work by someone
a long time ago or so his father said
but who it was he did not remember,
it was before his time.

But there comes a moment, there always does,
when a man stops his work, lays down his tools,
looks out over the dry brown distance
and wonders when they will come, the ones
the wall is meant for. At that moment
he sees between earth and sky
a cloud of dust like the drifting spores
of a puffball exploded by a foot.

He knows there is nothing to do but wait,
nothing he can do but stand on the wall. Everything
is in order, the wall as perfect as a man
can make it. It does not occur to him
that the cloud might be only a cloud of dust,
something the wind has raised out of nothing
and which will return to nothing. For a moment
he wonders what will happen when they come.
Will they honour him for his work, the hours
and years he has spent? But which side
of the wall do they come from?
No one has ever told him what would happen.

He will have to tell his son, he thinks,
his wife. He wishes his father were alive
to see them coming, but he is not,
and his son, who has already learned
the secrets of stone, is asleep.
It is a day to remember.
In all his life he has never been more
afraid, he has never been happier.

THERE IS A TIME

There is a time when the world is hard,
the winters cold and a woman
sits before a door, watching through wood
for the arrival of a man. Perhaps a child is ill
and it is not winter after all. Perhaps
the dust settles in a child's breath,
a breath so fragile it barely exists.
Tuberculosis or pneumonia. Perhaps
these words place her there, these words
naming the disease and still not curing it.

Maybe it is not the man she waits for.
We want it to be someone. We want
someone to relieve this hour. On the next farm
the nearest woman to the woman is also sitting
in dust or cold and watching a door. She is no help.
So let it be the man. He is in the barn
watching the breathing of his horses.
They are slow and beautiful,
their breath almost freezing in perfect clouds.
Their harness hanging down from the stalls
gleams, although old and worn. He is old and worn.
The woman is waiting behind the door
but he is afraid to go there because of her eyes
and the child who is dying.

There is a time when it is like this,
When the hours are this cold, when the hours
are no longer than a bit of dust in an eye,
a frozen cloud of breath, a single splinter in a door
large enough to be a life it is so small and perfect.
Perhaps there are soldiers coming from far away,
their buttons dull with dust or bright with cold,
though we cannot imagine why they would come here,
or a storm rolling down from the north
like a millwheel into their lives.

Perhaps it is winter.
There is snow. Or it could be dust.
Maybe there is no child, no man, no woman
and the words we imagined have not been invented
to name the disease there is no child to catch.
Maybe the names were there in a time before them
and they have been forgotten. For now let them die
as we think of them and after they are dead
we will imagine them alive again,
the barn, the breath, the woman, the door.

A RED BIRD BEARING ON HIS BACK AN EMPTY CUP

For Lorna

It was almost night when I asked the land
to hold in the folds of her bright skin
my body, save me from the wind. But I
have asked for abstinence before. The sun
broke against the land, its death
a witness to the thing I found:
a red bird bearing on his back an empty cup.
His eyes were blind. This is not fear.
I have spoken of prophecy before.
Silence is not the end.

I was walking the long hills in search
of forgiveness. I found the red bird
though all the signs warned me to be gone.
There was a rising moon. It was then
I disturbed your troubled sleep.
And then the grey dog, thin, and you
beside me, sick, grieving for innocence.
The dog carried with him the foreleg
of a deer; the hoof, the flesh still
hanging from the bone, the tired flesh.

Forgive me, I am almost old.
I was dreaming of my father in the garden
when winter was upon us, his rueful laugh.
The years have been long for us too, and winter.
It was finding the blind bird and his cup.
His burden seemed a consolation. He was why
I lifted you from sleep and led you
through the fences and scrub willow.
Perhaps there is a perfect detachment.
God knows, I want to believe in things.

I will list here what occurred: the bird
bearing on his back an empty cup, the dog,
the foreleg of the deer, your sleeping
and your rising, the pain I feel
when you are sick to death, my father,
all the things that swing into the mind
when I am tired of praise. It will always be now
when you read this poem. It will be new
and you and the nights and the long day gone.
Perhaps to name is excellence enough.

I will not speak again of death, though
I want death. There are many ceremonies.
I have not come through but there is
a quietness. It is not for nothing we love.
Even though winter is upon us and all
the signs warned me to be gone, though
my trespass will be called to account,
it is no matter. We are here to praise
the occurrences, the moment when a red bird
bears upon his back for us an empty cup.

WILD BIRDS

Because the light has paled and the moon
has wandered west and left the night
to the receding sea we turn into ourselves
and count our solitudes. The change
we might have wished for had we time

to wish is gone. The sacrifice of hours
has endured and we remember nothing of our days.
Neither the hand with the knife nor human gift
is enough to bring fulfillment. Form that was never
ours, the questioning of paradise, the beauty of

our minds. Once beyond the sight of land
I saw a flock of crows battle the wind.
Baffled, returning, knowing the landfall,
they beat their wings against a strength
greater than their own. We are all of us

as those birds I saw at sea blown outward
against our will. I read the books
and dreamed the dream that words could change
the vision, make of man a perfect animal
and so transformed become immortal.

What else was there to dream? Not this,
not this beating against the wind. Chaos
is our creation and the god we wished was man:
to turn again into the thing we are, yet be
black cinders lost at sea, the wild birds failing.

DOMINION DAY DANCE

The night is summer
and the hour is heavy with air that moves
like a slow mouth in the leaves of the chestnut,
the branches of the elms.
A boy dances in their shadows.
Across the street in the Legion Hall
music falls upon the dancers.
As the boy moves he imagines
a girl whose breasts
are small perfect pains on her chest
and he wants to touch them.
He has sworn tonight to dance
with a girl who is beautiful.
He does not know his desire
to never be alone again
is the beginning of loneliness.
It is a new kind of fear.
It has entered him like a cage enters
an animal, this thing his body does
moving in awkward grace
with nothing in its arms.

THE HAPPY LITTLE TOWNS

Walking the muddy road past the swamp
I thought the butterflies a gift I couldn't bear,
there in the sun pulling light into their wings,
drinking sweet water with their tongues.
I was so young I thought I was a man
and that little town a place where a life could be
made, that things like bears or ravens
or the body of a woman were sufficient to themselves
and without guile. That the man walking beside me
had a boot full of blood was nothing more
than the end of a day. A man who had opened
his body with an axe. It could have easily been
a boy with an eye scooped out, or a woman
bleeding into diapers for a month, afraid
to tell her man she'd lost his child.

That was the year my wife slept with my best friend.
I could tell her now the summer was oblivion,
that the blood gone from a body cannot be
given back, the wound opening like a mouth
without forgiveness. The inside of the body
when it first feels air feels only noise, as the
butterfly when it first crawls out of itself
feels only wonder and never eats again. I remember
the brightness of the days as my hands healed
the many injuries, the hours alone. It wasn't sadness
or self-pity, only oblivion, the kind a boy feels
when he is made into a man, wanting only to be
held, for the first time in his life without love.

The wreckage of that world stayed wreckage, though
we tried to build it back. The steady years of trying,
her taking the flowers I picked in the fields
and placing them in a jar where we watched them die.
What I remember most is that injured man who,
with the dignity of the very poor, told me he was
sorry to bother me, as if his wound could have waited
for a better time to happen; my hands putting him
back together, the stitches climbing up his leg
like small black insects I created out of nothing,
the curved steel needle entering his pale flesh,
pulling behind it a thread thin as a butterfly's
tongue, him saying he was sorry, and me knowing
for the first time in my life what that must mean.

WEASEL

Thin as death,
the dark brown weasel slides
like smoke through night's hard silence.
The worlds of the small are still. He glides
beneath the chicken house. Bird life
above him sleeps in feathers as he creeps
among the stones, small nose testing every board
for opening, a hole small as an eye, a fallen knot,
a crack where time has broken through.
His sharp teeth chatter.
Again and again he quests the darkness
below the sleeping birds. A mouse freezes,
small mouth caught by silence in the wood.
His life is quick. He slips into his hole.
Thin as death, the dark brown weasel slides
like smoke. His needles worry wood.
The night is long.
Above him bird blood beats.

NIGHT

In the bright room where Albinoni's adagio
plays its endless variations, my friends,
the few who know what silence is
and know this music is the pain
Alden Nowlan felt as he stumbled toward death
alone, blundering against the walls, I keep
the ivory *netsuke* and the fragment of blue
tile from the baths of Caracalla.
When I tell them of the musk of the flower
that bloomed for one short night in summer
they understand. The cactus sings to me.
I have these things to share. The ephemeral
moves among us, delicate as Cavafy's phrase:
like music that extinguishes far-off night.
I think of that phrase in my study, how
it moves among the things that are mine:
the scarred jade lion I bought for nothing in Xian,
the photograph of my father, the quiet one taken
when he was young in Europe in 1943,
and my poems, the broken ones that will never
be seen. These I keep for myself. They are
the other silence, the one that sings to me
when my friends are gone and the night
moves with great slowness in my hands.

DOSTOEVSKY

1.
A dead mouse on a forest path, ants and flies
sharing the feast. He can understand that.
He can understand the young crows
stumbling in the branches of a tree,
feathers not ready for flight. Bewildered,
innocent, the young do not know fear. This
makes him afraid, makes him want
to catch one, to slit its tongue
so it will speak in the language of crows,
the language of translation, the first chapter
of *Crime and Punishment*, the last chapter
of *The Idiot*. He knows he is mad. He does not
need the crescent moon to tell him this,
he does not need to hide in the trees,
a pale criminal watching the beautiful
young monk in the monastery garden
take a single strawberry from the field
and eat it very slowly as he walks to vespers.
Can a woman write about a man?
A man a woman?
Tristan and Isolde. There are too many
things in his mind. Who is Dostoevsky?
He wants to answer that. He is in retreat
playing Patience. It is a solitary game
played only in retreat, everything ordained,
everything in the turn of a card. The monk is
a crow in his black gown. Dostoevsky.

2.

A young man who is a dealer of *Chemin de Fer*
is rooted in the body of a German dowager.
He lifts a heavy breast covered in sweat
and puts it in his mouth. *Amor. Eros.*
His lips are the skin of a dead mouse.
He does not know why this has occurred
to him. He is thinking of Dostoevsky
and he knows nothing can be redeemed by this
image. Christ, he thinks, they must have smelled
at the gaming tables, their bodies unwashed,
drenched in perfume and pearls. Dostoevsky
gambling with the rich dowagers at a spa
in Germany, losing everything and wanting
to lose again. The game is *Chemin de Fer*.
It is the Nineteenth Century after Christ.
Prince Myshkin is singing.

3.

When he was a small boy he sat on the floor
gazing at the crotch of his mother's friend.
She was talking with his mother of the heat
and she opened her legs, her dress a blue flower
draped across her knees. Tea and matrimonial cake.
He thought an animal was biting her.
Sweat and gambling at a spa in Germany.
To turn great beauty into loss, to lose
it all on the turn of a card. Dostoevsky.
He thought an animal was biting her.
She smiled down at him knowing that pearls
were not drops of dew, were not the milky
semen floating in the menstrual sea.
Manichaean heresies. The blood and body
of Christ. A monk eating a strawberry.

4.

In Germany the dowagers wear pearls
if they are rich and fat and German
and they are gambling in a casino
during the Season in the Nineteenth Century.
Raskolnikov is sweating in his room.
Natasha is about to laugh.
An animal eats her.

5.

He is playing a game called Patience
and he does not want to think.
Everything hurts him.
The young monk walking to vespers,
a strawberry in his mouth. A dead mouse.
Crows singing Russian songs.
She eats matrimonial cake knowing
A child is looking up her dress.
Is that why she parts her legs?
Or is it just the heat?
Meanwhile the game is Patience
as the monks sing in high clear voices
the *Salve Regina* in the last hour,
vespers over and the compline begun.
Crows stumble in the trees
while their mother screams
and Dostoevsky thrashes in his room,
his wife forcing a stick into his mouth
to stop him from biting off his tongue.

WINTER 1

The generosity of snow, the way it forgives
transgression, filling in the many betrayals
and leaving the world
exactly as it was. Imagine a man
walking endlessly and finding his tracks,
knowing he has gone in a circle. Imagine
his disappointment. See how he strikes out again
in a new direction, hoping this way
will lead him out. Imagine how much
happier he will be this time with the wind
all around him, the wind filling in his tracks.

He is thinking of that man,
of what keeps him going.
The thought of snow,
small white grains sifting
into the holes where his feet went,
filling things in,
leaving no room for despair.

WINTER 4

He is thinking of the end of Oedipus,
not the beginning, not the part
where Oedipus chooses by giving the answer
to the beast at the Gate of Thebes.
No, it is the end he likes. The part
just after he puts out his eyes
and stands, suddenly
in that certain darkness, decided.

It is not a story of winter
but of the sun, the ceaseless
perfection of the desert in Africa.

How different it would be
had it taken place here, he thinks.
Here the critical moment
would be putting the eyes back
in their sockets, that first shock
exactly the same as in the other story
only the beginning would have
to be different, all the roles
reversed.

WINTER 13

There is a brief thaw and now
everything is frozen. Outside
ptarmigan wander ceaselessly
trying to find a way back
to where they believe
there is release from cold.
Beneath them their white sisters
struggle under the clear crust.
In the rare moments
when they are still
they are mirrors of each other,
each of them dying, each of them
wanting the other's dilemma,
believing the cries of the others
are lies, something done
only to torment them.

WINTER 16

Everything moves without change. The trees
without leaves dance sadly, allowing
nothing to get in their way. Not sorrow,
not snow under snow, but a slow forgetting.
The old moon sleeps with the young moon in her arms.
Words like that are like reaching out
in the darkness, wanting
to sleep and not being able to. Reaching out
to find nothing at the end of the hand but cold.
Wondering at flesh, its need, as the trees
who do not remember leaves, dance sadly
with a steady dumb grief, their dark moving
a monotonous music in the snowy night.

WINTER 20

Winter is not Colville, not that violent sentiment
without feeling, control without grief.
He is not how we imagine it. We are not
his model of intolerance, that accuracy
which is performance designed to instruct.
Imagine the space in falling snow
left behind by a woman
when she is walking through a storm.
We think it chaos,
but it is only presence reduced to intrusion.
Another order, which is what he praises.
It is soapstone before the carver
lifts his chisel, the form before form,
desolation without regret. Propriety
in a space made alien by the thought.
The answer to the question:
But what does it mean?
The old Eskimo laughing at such a strange request.

WINTER 33

The brightness which is the light seen from a tomb
and which is what the dead see when they gaze
with their marble eyes from the dark rooms they are
laid in. This is a whole city this snow.

WINTER 35

One is about the man who walks out into the storm
and is never seen again. We all know that one.
It is the story about grief and music,
where all the dancing is an escape
from virtue, everyone shaken by a higher crime,
the emptiness that follows completion,
the one the body knows
in the formal gentleness of suffering, everything gone,
everything forgiven in the land East of Eden.

Then there is the other story, the one
where the man enters out of the storm,
ice melting from his beard, his huge hand
moving over the fire, the fear of what will follow,
the women quiet, filling his cup and bowl
with all the food there is in hope it will be
enough, in hope he will be satisfied only with that,
and knowing he won't, knowing
this is the part of the story the reader will call
the middle, and hoping for an alternative, another
beginning, and ending it
before the mind reaches the end
with everyone crying out, everyone
saying things like: *Lie down in sorrow!*
or: *This is the burden of Babylon*

There is another story, there always is.
The one about...
of course, of course.
How cold it is with only a lamp in this small room.

WINTER 40

She is a northern woman, barely more
than a child, one who has walked through the drifts
to find her dream vision. Her eyes are
covered by a blade of bone, a thin slit
cut in it so the light does not blind her.
The man she has found is not one of the four
possibilities: father, brother, lover, son.
He is the dream man, given to her by the snow.

He has wandered far from the sea,
his crew dead, his ship broken in the ice.
If there were someone there to translate his song
it would start with the words: *At last.*
But only she is there.
As he sings she cuts off his fingers,
only these small bones and the twenty-six
teeth for her necklace.

They will be her medicine, something
to shake over the bellies of women
in childbirth, the heads of men
who have returned empty from hunting,
their minds become snow.

How like a real man he is, she thinks.
How real this dream, the blood on the ice.
How thin he is, how much like the snow is his flesh.

THE KILLER

I have spent too many of my years in you,
have sat inside your body in the bars
while you drank your solitary beers,
their wet circles somehow making sense to me,
the way they almost touched each other
as you lifted the glass to your lips
and drank. I have risen with you
and gone to your truck where the Winchester
rested in its rack and driven through
the country, down the dusty roads,
past the creeks and willows
where grouse and pheasants find their lives
in the quiet thickets. I have stopped
with you and waited for nothing.
I have stepped from that truck
and stood in the gravel, have reached down
for the stone and picked it up and hurled it
at nothing. I have gotten back into the truck
and driven into town past the many friends
and enemies and stopped. I have taken
the rifle from its rack and aimed it
through the window and pressed the trigger,
felt that soft blow in the shoulder
as the rifle recoiled.
                          I have travelled through
the air, through a window, through a wall,
and through my father's chest into his heart, and
I have stayed, a small thing lodged there,
and felt the blood that made me
heave into silence. I have spent most of my life
with you, you whose name I do not know,
you who drove away, leaving
my body inside that heart
lifting up the many pieces, unable
to put any of them together, surrounded
by my father's blood, and wanting
not to be there, wanting only
to be with you, riding quietly
into whatever it was you knew.

THE FAR FIELD

We drove for more than an hour, my father's hands
on the truck's wheel, taking us farther and farther
Into the hills, both of us watching
the sagebrush and spare pines drift
past, both of us silent. He did not know
what to do with me. I think he thought of
my death, as a man will whose son has chosen
to destroy. I think that's why he drove
so long, afraid to stop for fear
of what he'd do. My mother had cried
when we left, her hands over her mouth,
saying through her splayed fingers
my father's name, speaking
that word as if it were a question. I
sat there peaceful with him,
knowing for these hours he was wholly mine.

He stripped me naked in the last hour of day
and made me stand with my back to him, my bare
feet in the dust, my back and buttocks to him,
a naked boy, hands braced upon the hood,
staring across the metal at the hills.

I remember the limb of the tree falling
upon me, the sound of the white wood crying
as it hurt the air, and the flesh of my body
rising to him as I fell to the ground and rose
only to fall again. I don't remember pain,
remember only what a body feels
when it is beaten, the way it resists
and fails, and the sound of my flesh.

I rose a last time, my father dropping
the limb of the tree beside me.
I stood there in my bones wanting it not to be
over, wanting what had happened to continue, to go
on and on forever, my father's hands on me.

It was as if to be broken was love, as if
the beating was a kind of holding, a man
lifting a child in his huge hands and throwing him,
high in the air, the child's wild laughter
as he fell a question spoken into both their lives,
the blood they shared pounding in their chests.

FATHERS AND SONS

I will walk across the long slow grass
where the desert sun waits among the stones
and reach down into the heavy earth
and lift your body back into the day.
My hands will swim down through the clay
like white fish who wander in the pools
of underground caves and they will find you
where you lie in the century of your sleep.

My arms will be as huge as the roots of trees,
my shoulders leaves, my hands as delicate
as the wings of fish in white water.
When I find you I will lift you out
into the sun and hold you
the way a son must who is now
as old as you were when you died.
I will lift you in my arms and bear you back.

My breath will blow away the earth
from your eyes and my lips will touch
your lips. They will say the years have been
long. They will speak into your flesh
the word *love* over and over,
as if it was the first word of the whole
earth. I will dance with you and you
will be as a small child asleep in my arms
as I say to the sun, bless this man who died.

I will hold you then, your hurt mouth curled
into my chest, and take your lost flesh
into me, make of you myself, and when you are
bone of my bone, and blood of my blood,
I will walk you into the hills and sit
alone with you and neither of us
will be ashamed. My hand and your hand.

I will take those two hands and hold them
together, palm against palm, and lift them
and say, this is praise, this is the holding
that is father and son. This I promise you
as I wanted to have promised in the days
of our silence, the nights of our sleeping.

Wait for me. I am coming across the grass
and through the stones. The eyes
of the animals and birds are upon me.
I am walking with my strength.
See, I am almost there.
If you listen you can hear me.
My mouth is open and I am singing.

THE ATTITUDE OF MOURNING

He had walked out of the Pitti Palace into the rain, thinking
of that painting of Franz Hals' high in the corner
where the light was dimmest, its anonymity intact.
The one of the young girl in the attitude of mourning.
She had reminded him of the vulture he had seen
in South America years ago, the one that huddled
under the geraniums during the rain,
not blinking, its two dark wings
pegged through the cardinal joints to the ground
while everything above it flowered red.
The rain striking its naked head.
But that was years ago when he was young.
Back then he had thought he understood
the magnitude of such an exile.

But this was not Medellin, it was
Florence with all its clarity intact,
its opulence a kind of tired memory, malignant
as light when it struggles with the rain
in the winter of Italy. It is the same
light an apple contains that rots from the inside,
that slow umber growing from the center
toward the beauty the skin inhabits.

That is what art is, he thought, the perversity
of wanting that, the choosing of innocence
as a model for loss. He imagined the stained hands
of Franz Hals, their sureness as they removed
the young girl's shift, the light
from the northern window, the girl's mother
at the door counting the money
the canvas ready, the brush and the other brushes.

Later that night the palace was what he had wanted,
the walls rotting, the frescoes crumbling. The woman there
was all flesh, someone who simply wanted less.
This century would never paint her.
He looked at her breasts and her long wrists
and understood that pleasure when it becomes cruelty
is inward, a kind of bruise the body grows,
and knew then
he wasn't speaking of her but of himself.

Do you want me to hurt you? he asked.
No, she said, *non c'e necessita*,
her dialect peculiar, so that the host,
the large Englishman with the bare red feet
who had been talking of his mother and her distaste,
how she had told him when he was still a boy
she had slept with his father
only once, unsuccessfully, told me I should ignore her.
She is from Rome, he said. *And they know nothing in Rome.*

THE BOOK OF KNOWLEDGE

He had been reading volume seven of *The Book of Knowledge*
and he got to thinking about those fakirs,
the difference between one nail and a thousand,
so he had taken his mother's sewing basket
and slowly, with what he thought then was patience,
took her needles and shaking only a little,
pushed them slowly through the skin
of his left arm, in and then out, the nine needles
resting there in a row, the flesh white and hard.
There was very little blood.
He pulled his sleeve over them
and went down to breakfast, his father quiet
as he drank his coffee, his sister watchful,
his brothers arguing over the last bits of meat.
Each time he lifted his fork
he could feel the fabric of his sleeve
catch at the needles, his flesh moving.
Sitting there he realized for the first time
how dangerous he was.

THE FIREBREATHER

In memory of Marcel Horne

She took him to the shed in the field behind the house.
For six days he had sat there naked in the darkness without food
while the water he was allowed went slowly bad
in the New Mexico heat. On the last day the gypsy woman
came in and told him she was tired of his impatience.
She began to talk of her day, the morning in the market,
her husband's drinking, her daughter's whoring
after a Mexican businessman who sold melons in Texas.
While she spoke she began to light wooden matches,
striking them on a flat stone she held on her lap.
She sat very close to him and as each match flared
she would hold it to his skin, sticking it there,
the match burning, the smell of his own flesh.
He looked at his arms and chest, the way
the match would sometimes burn all the way
to the end and not fall off, the match curling,
those black stems sticking from him like fragile quills.
This went on for a long time until he no longer remembered
what he was there for, the sweat from his face and shoulders
running down his body, that sweet salt touching his wounds.
Then she opened his mouth, burning his tongue and lips.
The pain you feel is the pain of the outward, she said.
Later I will teach you the other pain.
When you have learned that you will be ready
to breathe fire.

BALANCE

He watched the horses come, huge in the afternoon,
their rubber hooves a dull sound under the screaming,
the riders swinging clubs to the right and left.
As he watched he saw a woman with a child go down
under a black horse, the horse careful not to step on her
as the rider leaned like a polo player
and struck her across the shoulders as she fell.
The horse and rider looked like they had practiced this
a long time, the rider balanced perfectly,
the horse moving as if without effort, though
he could see the great muscles moving under its skin,
the crowd splintering into the many
narrow streets that led from the Avenida del Sol.
He had always remembered that, the horse's gentleness,
so strange in a body that large, the rider's steady grace,
and the woman
rising after they passed over, the look on her face,
the baby crying, the street almost empty, people
stepping from doorways to sit at the tables again,
the waiters bringing wine and beer.

DINNER

I would like to have dinner with the man
who didn't follow Christ, the one who,
when Jesus said: *Follow me and I
will make you fishers of men*, decided
to go fishing instead, getting in his boat,
pushing out from shore, his nets clean
and repaired, thinking I will have to work
even harder now in order to feed
everyone left behind. I would like
to sit on the beach with him
in front of a careful fire,
his wife and children asleep,
sharing a glass of wine, both of us
telling stories about what we'd done
with our lives, the ones we caught,
the ones that got away.

THE CHANGING ROOM

In the changing room our naked bodies moved
from our dark cubicles to stand in a circle
around a rusted grate where the slippery water
heavy with sweat and steam sank into a hole.
On the other side of the wall we heard
the girls, their screams, their crazy laughter,
the high wild madness of summer at the lake.
Listening, we passed among ourselves the picture
of a woman on her knees holding a man in her mouth.
Her eyes were closed. I remember that, remember
thinking it was what she held that made her blind,
remember the look on the man's soft face,
a flat pale stare that made him somehow missing
as if at the centre of himself he wasn't there.
I knew even then there was a holiness to it
and would have called it icon had I known the word.
As the picture moved among us we circled
the heavy grate, our bodies hunched
emptying ourselves in that white silence.

We changed then and ran into the light,
banging against the girls who came out
from the other side. I wondered
if the girls had a picture, the man in it
blind as the woman was in ours? Would he be
on his knees and if he was what of a woman's
did he hold in his heavy mouth?
As the bodies of my friends
scattered across the sand, I climbed under the pier
where Margery stood in her cotton dress.
We undressed on the dark sand and stared
at each other. I used to dream her on her knees,
holding me in her mouth. I imagined
the look of the standing man, practised
his vacant stare as my body poured into her.

When we were dressed I walked her through the alleys
and stood with her under the elms at her mother's shack,
our bodies almost touching, our secrets safe, staring
beyond ourselves at what I thought must be the same
imagining: each of us on our knees, each of us
holding each other in our mouths, though what I held
in mine I didn't know, and with her eyes an emptiness,
I heard her mother calling her to home,
knew my own was somewhere calling me,
and ran with the last light back to my flesh,
my supper waiting, my mother at the stove, my father
silent, all of us eating the food that she had made.

COUGAR

The cougar before she falls from her high limb
holds for one moment the ponderosa pine, her back
arched, her tail so still the forest stops.
There are silences to learn,
each one an invocation: the one that follows
a father's rage at a child, a woman's rage at man,
a child's tears you watch as if the sound
was a language you must learn. But a cougar's falling?
Nothing is so quiet. Even the wind stops to listen.
Beetles, busy at death, lift up their jointed legs,
whiskey-jacks slide quietly away, and ravens appear
as if they had been made from the air.
It is to watch a thing whose only gift is death
give to herself, feeling the explosion in her heart
a thing she has made and not the men below
and not the dogs as they watch her falling
through the limbs and then erupting into sound,
their hard mouths biting what is already dead.
It is the boy on a horse so old it will not run,
a boy who watches, not understanding the men
who, when she falls, shoot their rifles at the sun,
as if with such exultance
they could bring a darkness into the world.

THE CALF

In the orchard they had tied the calf between two trees
and, because they wanted to please, knowing
he was from the town and knew about books and songs
they offered her to him first.
He didn't understand and refused, standing there
awkward in his town shoes and ironed pants.
The boys laughed at him then and dropped their jeans,
taking turns, one hand gripping the curved
bone of her hip, the other holding in a fist
her tail to the side, their white buttocks
pumping in the sun. When they were done they were angry
though he wasn't sure at what or whom. Perhaps they thought
he had disdained the gift, or disdained them.

They turned from him then,
going through the apple trees to the fields,
their narrow backs changing from shadow into light.
Alone, walking back to the summer farm, he was afraid,
the trees heavy with green fruit in the heat,
the swollen grass breaking with pollen
against his legs, covering him with dust.

Later the last of summer would give him Emma's breasts
in the snake-grass meadows below the swimming-hole
and in the deserted barn, Irene's mouth, wet and warm,
but he thinks now only of the boys
and their offering, how he had failed
something or someone, the boys moving slowly, shuffling
sullen away from him.
                        The calf had snuffled the thick grass,
still tied, and when he released her thinking she would run,
she didn't move away, instead
bunted him softly, the hair around her budding
horns curled and white
where he placed his hands, he thought then
to hold her away, holding her in the way
light is held when it does not come from the sun.

WISTERIA

You say wisteria and something plunders you,
a mouth heavy with blue
as if it had spent the morning eating grapes
or the heavy black cherries of childhood you picked
wild in the alien orchards of the desert hills. Words
come flowering, myriad
as if they grew in clusters on your tongue, as if
you were speaking to the grandmother
you never knew who sat
strapped in a chair for the last years of her life
asking for fruit from a tree that wasn't there.
Hers was a kind of frailty, tough and trembling,
like a scant branch you think if you take
will break. She wanted
fruit for the pies they wouldn't let her make.

A trembling, as wisteria, or hands when you are still
a child that reach farther than they can to plunder
a distant branch of its first fruit. Still,
inside that old woman I never knew was a stone
as there was inside my mother. Cherries,
she would cry, cherries, and I would go to her
if I could, my mouth a rich purple,
and speak to her of the hills
and the solitary lark beyond the wisteria
real as the knife she holds as she peels
the skin I wear like a shroud, whispering
through whatever blood there is:
you must eat child, you must eat.

CHINA WHITE

He sat in the small room thinking of geraniums,
that crowded red as close to blood
as any flower is. It was after Archie offered her
to him, saying, *Anything you want,*
and her on the bed, nodding off, the exact particular
in her mind a shell she might ride on without menace.
Her blonde hair was another kind of light.
When he declined, Archie covered her again, his hand
hesitating just a moment as the blanket fell, a quietness
he tried to understand. All this for some China white.
Sometimes you can't imagine what it's like, given
such magic as occurs in time. What is in his mind
are geraniums, those bloody flowers
rising from their arms into the last syringe,
and the ones his mother grew so many years ago
beside the stones covered in red lichens.
Such textures as there are in the many
gardens we make from ourselves. Then, leaving,
going out into whatever beauty he can find.

MOTHS

The air breathes like a tree just before dawn
and my hands that rested on your body
when they held your sleeping, move away from me,
and fly like moths with only night
to guide them, go with their wings to the sea.
Who I am falls behind and all I can see
are the dead who have gathered here to free
this hour from the many hours.

Pale moths, soft birds of the night,

move among their grey faces, touch
their small shy feet, cleanse what must be
cleansed in this dark where the dead have come
for blessing. Touch their lips
with your wings so they may sing.
Be to them what the heart is when it sleeps.

THE BARE PLUM OF WINTER RAIN

The instrument of your poverty
is an infinite departure, the hawk unseen
until you see him without prey
in the bare plum of winter rain.
He rests inside hunger
and he does not sing today.
How rare the gesture we make
with nothing. It is of the spirit and without
value. The bare plum, the winter rain
and the hawk seeing what you cannot say.
These steady accretions, yet allowing them
to stay as you stay with music after music
plays, and of course there is always,
always hunger, and, of course, poverty,
and the bare plum, empty, and the rain.

THE OLD ONES

For Al Purdy

He thought of the horses in January,
the old ones who had stopped moving
and stood away from the wind
in the leached coulee above Six Mile Creek,
snow and wind scouring their matted backs
and he wonders now what they dreamed
in the dead cold of that winter years ago.
Were they the horses who had loved
the steady pull of trace and strain, the long
journey in from Six Mile, buckboards
and wagons resting grey under the trees
in late summer, still hitched, standing
in the bare shade without water, waiting?
It was winter when he saw them last,
the old ones in the wind, their great heads
bent to spare grasses in the bleached coulee.
He had watched the wind crawl
through the horses' manes and tails
Even then he knew he'd seen the last
of their long journey to the town,
the blacksmith shop shut down,
the trees where they were tied
a lot for cars and trucks. The old ones
in their last winter, the ones who loved
the wagons and buckboards,
the steady sound of hooves in the dust,
the men and women and children behind them
talking their way to the stores and bars,
the hitching rails on Main Street, all that time
gone now. Still, they must have dreamed
or maybe it was only him,
balanced on his haunches in a frieze of wild rose
staring down at them and taking his body
among them for a moment,
snow cutting his eyes, the wind not yet
ready to die in those sagebrush hills
where the coulee lay below Six Mile
and the old ones waiting for it to end.

THE WARD CAT

The man in the hospital who, late
in the night, the women, sick, asleep
took off his clothes, folding them neatly
and laying them down, the shirt and pants,
the socks and underwear, and the shoes
side by side beside the white chrome chair,
in a room with only a small light
burning above each bed, lifted
the covers and lay down
beside his wife who had not wakened
for two years from the coma, and
placing his arm across her breasts,
his leg upon her leg, closed his eyes,
silent, still, the breathing of his wife,
his arm rising and falling with her life
while the ward cat who would sleep
only with her, watched from
the foot of the bed, one ear forward
and the other
turned to the sounds of the distant city.

THE MADBOY

Every day the madboy runs
up the street from the Home,
his heavy feet hard on the pavement,
his arms flailing, his blond hair
wild in the sun. He has slipped
from some door or window,
some crack in the wall only he knows
and now is free to run. As he goes
he keeps looking back at his pursuers
who follow him into the sun.
In the boy's face is both glee and terror.
He knows they will catch him.
They always do.
If there is fear it is the thought
they won't come after him
and will go on making breakfast,
flipping pancakes and bacon
for the other boys locked
in the bodies of men who crowd
the morning table at the Home
and he will finally make it to the corner
and be free. It is the place he never gets to.
The boy slows as his pursuers come on.
They walk slowly in the morning,
quiet, tired, knowing this is just
the beginning of another day,
and the boy will wait for them just short of where
the road breaks. And now he is happy
as they hold him in their hands.
He laughs at the run he's made again,
his face lifted up into the sun reflects
the knowledge he knows is his,
that for him the only escape is surrender,
that giving himself up is his whole life
and the room they will take him to
is a place where he can hold himself
sure of the great journey he has made,
bound once again by a locked door and the glass
in a window where he can see himself
among the thousand cells of wire embedded there,
knowing in his single mind there is nowhere to go
but into the arms of those who want to hold us.

LOOKOUT

Sometimes you look out over the great plains
and see a faint light falling between what we think are mountains.
It is then you know you are living far away from the world.
As the abandoned hulk of a turtle you found once in a field
far from water. How you squatted on your bare heels and stared at the bulk
of that green dome. The body a thought inside that emptiness.
Or the night you stood by the redwood tree on the street outside your home
and stared through the burden of heavy needles at your wife
as she stared out of the light. How for one moment you were afraid.
Sometimes we live far away from the world,
bright sunlight, a heavy dark. Without thought, and waiting.

INFIDELITY

Under the rain, under the spare trunks of Indian plum,
the faded rust of redwood needles and the club moss
grown thick from the winter feast of weather. On his knees
he picks the flat needles splayed there, gathering them
in the way he remembers the monk in the old garden
gathering, his quiet in Kyoto, and leaning down after sweeping
with a bamboo rake and picking up a single needle,
placing it on a swept pile, then turning, going up
a worn path that followed the thin creek, and gone.
It was so much what he had imagined in the old poems
of Issa, a kind of stillness, perfection being
what distracts us in the moment, something forgotten
in the ordinary harmony we strive for and almost reach.
That is why he is on his knees cleaning the garden.
He is thinking of his dream, how he was gentle with her,
touching only the curve of hair above the pale shell
of her ear, the dampness there. And then the wind
and the going out into the last dark, and beginning
the clearing away, his eyes a mist, how he remembered
that, on his knees, one needle and then another, thinking
it is what the old know, a slight turning, something
not seen, and reaching back for what was left behind
on the moss, something fallen, under the rain.

THE SPOON

He has picked up the spoon from among all the small things
on the table, the knife and fork, the salt shaker you don't shake
but turn and grind, the bowl with its applesauce, the glass of milk,
and how he hesitated between the glass and the spoon, but chose
the spoon, and his daughter's voice going on
in a low and steady murmur, her blonde hair cut short
and the bit of gray at her temples,
and how he remembers his old mother hating flowers
after his father's funeral, how she would never have any
in the house, and his daughter still talking to him
in her quiet steady voice about things he already knows,
but knowing it is important for her to say them,
important for her to make some kind of order
out of what must seem to her the chaos of what will be
his life now, and the dog barking outside, and the light
on the table, and the spoon in his hands, and he turns it
over among his fingers and marvels at how his hands
have been holding spoons all his life, and he holds it
by the end of the handle and looks carefully into the shallow
bowl polished so carefully by his wife and sees there
his face upside down, and how if he could understand
the spoon everything would become clear to him, if he
could understand something this simple, something
so small and ordinary that he has used every day of his life
and never paid attention to until now, something very small,
and very simple, and not a glass, not a flower, just a spoon,
and that without it everything in his life
would have been different if there had never been spoons, this spoon,
and he feels a sense of wonder at what he holds, and he reaches out
and takes a spoonful of applesauce from the bowl in front of him
and gently, and very carefully lifts it not to his mouth,
but to his daughter's mouth, and he touches it against her lips
and she opens her mouth and it is very quiet now and the only thing
he knows he can do is in this moment, and that is what he does.

THE WAR

Afternoon, and the heat upon the table slipped across the Melmac plates
and the steel knives and the butter, melted from the plastic saucer, slipped
to the edge of the scarred pine table and sank to the linoleum. Heat
like the pale water you see on desert roads ahead of you, the shimmer
and the mirage of a lake reflected from the bellies of clouds. You drive
through thirsty, the wheel wet under your palms. Before us water glasses
beaded from the sweat of air when the cold meets it, the home-made beer
thin with foam. He lived above Swan Lake and made pottery there,
celadon and slip glazes drawn from the yellow clay cliffs, temmoku,
the rabbit's-fur black running down, feldspar, iron, copper, and the ashes
from bones, calcium and phosphorous, ball clays and kaolin, all
for his huge hands to make into the empty containers others filled
with flowers, the vitrified glass, what he was proud of, a frail red rising
out of a deeper brown, the black, the impurities, the polluting elements,
and the beauty of his making. He was German, come over after the war,
and the same age as me, his parents dead, I think, or if not dead
then never spoken of. His hand reached through the air for bread,
broke off the crust at the end, and then he ate it, slowly, between
sips of beer. We talked the way men talked back then when they spoke
of the past, a privacy only spoken to wives and rarely then, the older days
best kept where they were in the locked leather satchel of the heart.

His was a long story that came slowly out of silence
and told without his eyes looking at me, but staring instead
out the window at the stubborn apples ripening, a pale brush of fire
flaring under the hard green. Summer in the Okanagan. The heat
and a single fly he caught in the middle of the telling, his one hand
holding what was left of the bread and his other, the left one, coming
behind the fly and then sweeping slowly, catching the fly as it rose
backwards as flies do when they first lift from what they rest on, bread,
the crumbs fallen on the slick surface of the table, a lick of wet butter.
He held his fist to my ear so I could hear the buzzing
then flung the fly to the floor, the single sharp click of its body
breaking there. And the story going on, the fly an interruption
he seemed unaware of except for the holding it to my ear
to hear its frantic wings, its sharp death, and the bread almost gone.
I spoke of the war and how it had shaped who I was, the years
forming me, had told him of my childhood and my father

gone to fight in Europe and of my playing what we called
as children, War. How we would choose sides, the smallest kids
the enemy, the Germans, and how we would come down on them
with our wooden rifles made from broken apple boxes
and bayonet them where they lay exposed, choosing to ignore their cries
of, It's not fair. We pushed the thin blades of our rifles
into their soft bellies, their shouts and cries meaning nothing to us
and then their tears, shameless, little kids broken in the shallow trenches
we had made in the clay hills, imagining what our fathers did each day
in the sure glory they never spoke of afterward, no matter our begging.

And his story.

That he watched his father and uncle come home to their farm
in the Black Forest, the horses pulling the short wagon in the night,
nostrils breathing mist in the cold, the wagon back piled with straw.
And the bodies of children under the straw.
That they had hunted them down in the forest, children
run from the gathering of jews and gypsies, tattered clothes and rags
wrapped round their feet. He remembered the small feet hanging
from the back of the wagon, the rags like torn flags fluttering.
His father and uncle had lifted the bodies one by one and fed them
into the grinders with dry corn and rotting turnips and blackened potatoes,
the pigs clambering over each other and screaming.
His mother had found him watching and carried him back
into the house, swore him to silence, said what she said and said again,
and he had not spoken of it these past thirty years and why
he spoke of it now he did not know, but that I had asked him of the war,
and of children playing, and that he had played too, but what games
they were he didn't remember, it was so long ago, those years, that war.
But what he remembered most were the feet sticking out
from under the straw, the horses' heavy breathing, the rags fluttering,
and his father sitting beside his uncle, tired, staring into the dark barn,
and the wagon pulling heavy through the ruts,
and the rags wrapped around the feet sticking out from the straw,
and the rags fluttering. That. He remembered that.

In the desert hills the ponderosa pines have grown three hundred years
among bluebunch wheatgrass and cheatgrass and rough fescue, and
there are prickly-pear cactus in spring whose flowers are made one each day,

and among the grasses are rabbit-brush and sagebrush and antelope brush
where the mountain bluebird is a startled eye, the grasshopper sparrow,
and the sage thrasher, and the wood mouse and harvest mouse,
and the kangaroo rats who come out at night to feed on seeds and moths.
There are these living things, and they are rare now and not to be seen
except for the careful looking in what little is left of that desert place. And I
list them here in a kind of breathing, the vesper sparrow, the saw-whet owl,
and the western meadowlark, and the northern scorpion and the western rattlesnake,
now almost gone, the last of them slipped away into what I remember
of that time when I lived among them. I name only what I can,
my friend, the potter who lived above Swan Lake, who made pottery
from kaolin and ball clay and the glazes from the yellow clay of the hills,
and who was but a child in that far war almost no one remembers
now, the warriors dead, and the people dead, the men and women dead,
and the children dead, and the children of those warriors and those people
who remember are now fewer than they were, and that is how it is now.

Sage thrasher, wood mouse, western meadowlark, and saw-whet owl,
and the meadowlark, and the vesper sparrow, and rough fescue,
and I must tell you so you understand, that we sat there at that table
with cold glasses of beer and the remains of the bread we ate together
and he showed me how to cup my hand and come up slowly
behind a resting fly and then sweep my hand through the air
perhaps two inches from the table top, the fly who lifts backwards
when he flees, caught in my fist, and then flinging it to the floor, the click
of its body breaking there. And that I learned how to do that,
and it was important I knew what I was learning, though it was
only a kind of game between two men killing flies, and then
we went outside under the weight of the heavy sun and talked a moment,
and he did not speak of his crying at the table and I did not speak of it,
for we were men of that time and we had learned long ago not to speak
of tears and of the stories that bring them, and that in this only world
there are things that must be remembered, and that they be spoken of,
scarlet gilia, parsnip-flowered buckwheat, white-tailed jackrabbits,
and balsamroot, and the rare sagebrush mariposa, and all such things
that are almost gone, and that I can still catch a fly the way
he taught me, and that we stood there by his truck in the dust and the heat
and said nothing to each other, only stared out into the orchards
and the green apples ripening there, and then he was gone into the desert
and I can tell you only this of what I remember of that time.

THE GREEN DRESS

In the green dress, separate, the floor retreating
from her, so that it seemed she was farther away
than the others thought, around her white walls, severe,
and the doors white, and a single high window, a photo
on the wall of a horse's head, poorly taken, the light
wrong, the background cluttered, things
getting in the way, intruding, haphazard, and not
the fault of things themselves, the fragments,
old harness, a bale of hay, a man's shoulder,
his shirt with part of a floral pattern showing,
perhaps roses, and wrong. So the woman in the green dress
with her hands precisely on her knees, her face held up
so that her throat is exposed, the lines of the muscles drawn,
and her eyes, not closed, but open, and staring at the door
through which the undertaker will soon appear bearing in his hands
the ashes of her son in a plain white box, and her waiting
for that, the green dress not a special one, not one
she might wear every day, but a dress she nevertheless chose
and by such choice refused extremity, both simple and not,
reaching into the dark, and taking that dress from among
the many dresses and saying, terrible, yes, this one will do.

A WOMAN EMPTIES HER SOCK DRAWER

Her hands stir among thin socks, sheer silks and coloured cottons,
the low socks and the high, little rabbits and ducks that danced
around the circle of ankle bones, pansies and peonies
fading, the calf-high sheers, the thigh-high silks and nylons, the small,
delicate tears in the mesh, old scars where buttons had gripped them,
the faint discolourations where wine had been spilled, coffee and tea,
her hands remembering how they straightened out the long seams,
the faraway warmth now cooled, and then *this* into the bin, the bag,
and *that* refused and *these* discarded, the drawers emptying,
the scent of cedar and sandalwood faint on her fingertips,
the twist-ties bound, and finally the quiet as she pushed the drawer back
into the darkness of the chiffonier, the little baskets empty,
a single silk stocking on the throw-rug by the door, curled upon itself
like a tangled sentence read over and over again, and memorized, forgotten,
her hands that touched them once, withdrawn, the high thigh
and slender calf, the ankle, foot, the glance that saw the stocking
cross smooth over its sister, a faint musk still in its woven mesh.

THREADED BLOOD MOSS

He is sitting in the old silence, having given up memory again
in anticipation of inevitable decay, holes in the brain, hollow throngs.
He thinks about the steady dispensations, the old and the new,
the way small children used to shine after weeping, their faces
round with hope, and him knowing it won't be like that again.
Tattered Rag, Frog Pelt, Lettuce Lung, and the exquisite
Peppered Moon, him down on his knees, his eyes in the dawn
and naming the mosses no one knows anymore, the new children
afraid to touch anything. He remembers the white of his father's cheek,
the thin stiffness as of old china cups pushed to the back,
the thin brown lines inside caused by the crazing time makes
of things. How precious the broken. Who kisses the dead anymore?
Who cradles their slender fingers in their own, a hand
reaching out to touch cold flesh, the body just recently released
from the ice house, someone somewhere cleaning gas jets,
ashes and bits of bone crunching underfoot. He remembers his mother,
the opal ring lying on the ashes in the box he made to hold her.
The undertaker asked him if he wanted the ring to remain
inside. He said, yes, knowing as the undertaker went away to glue
the lid shut he would take the ring. Perhaps some child wears it
now, some girl, some woman, someone who loves the antique
setting. His hand brushes the Threaded Blood Moss, frail hairs
clinging to his rough palms. How afraid he was back then.
How impossible it was to remember: the polished grey slate
that he slipped upon when he tried to turn away, the heavy drapes
he blundered into as he fell backward into the mirror of himself.

WHAT MY FATHER TOLD ME

1.
The house was beside the sawmill and each morning
the floors were burdened with dust from the huge fires
that burned all night on the graveyard shift. The dust
blew through the cracks and crannies, the windows, doors,
through the broken places in the walls and roof. The dust
settled on the table and chairs, the crockery,
the children's beds, the worn blankets covering them, and them
trembling with each small breath they took, tremors of dust
rising from their mouths, thin, elusive trails in my wife's hair,
on her lips and cheeks. Standing by the bed in my bare feet
I stared at the dust in the cold of the winter night. Alive, it was
like smoke when it settled on snow, something grey
that crawled, writhing there on the white drifts
in the village, in that valley, in that winter, the mill
making its terrible music. A hurting song. You could call it
that, something a man might sing if he had lost
it all, his woman, his children, his truck, his job;
everything somehow broken, his life now strange and alone.

2.
Almost, I say, such songs as what we hear on empty roads
in the cold, the twisting ruts throwing us side to side, our hands
gripping the wheel for dear life. Not fear, just a machine
carrying us in the false, reflected light we call the moon
when it's alive on ice, and miles to go
before you get anywhere close to what you could
call home; singing along with the voice on the radio,
forgetting for hours it was you singing the song,
the radio not working in those mountains.

3.
The sound of the moon on snow is a whispering.
You hear it even when you know you can't,
humming the parts you don't know, the story that explains
everything, the refrain the one sure thing, and shouting it in the dark.

4.

My father was drunk. It was twelve at night and he had come in
out of the snow, my wife in her pyjamas and me in my underwear,
amazed he was there, in that village, in that storm, his heavy coat,
and the thin icicles melting in his hair. My wife poured him a glass of rye,
and he held it in his two hands, cupped there as if it was some fire
he thought could warm him. I know now my mother told him
to visit us. He'd been in the village for three days, drinking
with his army buddies, the ones who came back, the ones who
made it after the war. He didn't want to be with us. He'd risen
from whatever shack or cabin, house or hotel room, and stumbled
out into the night, knowing he had to go because she'd told him to,
my mother. *Visit the kids*, she must have said, and him nodding
as he went out the door. Did I say he didn't want to be there? Yes,
and though I knew he had been in our village those days and nights,
I never thought him possible in the hovel we called a home. The fires
from the burner rose from behind his head, the window drifted
with dust so the glow of the flames seemed muted, another kind of fire,
the one you grow inside, the one that smoulders,
peat fire, a brown-coal fire, wet wood, damp dust, smoke.
He had no idea what to say or do, lifted to his lips
the whiskey I'd been saving for the Christmas months away
and drank it down, a single swallow, his mouth then lax, his lips
hanging from his teeth, the ice melted from his hair, the snow too,
gone from his boots, a puddle at his feet eating into the throw rug,
my wife standing then, smiling, a little shy, and going back to bed,
saying nothing, a nod, the kids still sleeping, and me hearing the door
latch behind her, imagining her curled at the edge of the bed, as far
away from me as she could get, as she often did those last years,
a body I could never find. And then, just my father and I breathing.

5.

I don't know now why I asked him about the war, except
I knew he'd been with his army buddies, the ones who came back in '45 and '46,
young men gone cold inside, or so hot the nights burned them.
The years that followed, the silences, my mother telling us
not to talk to him, and not to ask anything. He looked down
into his glass as if he thought he could find something there,
a small drop or two left, shivering in the bottom,
the glass he lifted to his mouth and held there long enough
for one last drop to fall upon his tongue. *That war*, he mumbled.
And I waited for what he'd never said before,
my father's head blundering then on his thick neck, a steer come up
out of a chute to the killing floor, that kind of heaviness, brutal
in its anger, its innocence. And I could tell you of what he told me then,
his friend burning alive as he tried to climb from the turret of his tank,
another friend quickly buried somewhere in Holland, my father
thinking he'd go back and find him and never did,
and later the woman in the ruined house. *A German woman,*
he said, one they found in hiding in the basement rubble.
It was the way he said, *They had her,* and him looking slyly up at me,
a look that was complicit, that told me we were somehow
in the story together, that I was his son, a man now
though I was barely twenty-two, married, three children,
and I knew they had raped her, the German, that woman,
and my father seeing me staring at him,
and, angry, saying, *No,* that he'd waited outside,
and I knew, when his eyes slipped away, that he had lied.

6.

On the dusty floor were our three trails: the ones my wife made
coming in and going out, her trail to the kitchen and the bottle,
and the trail she took to my father when she gave him the drink,
the trail she followed when she left, the marks of her bare feet,
so small, one print perfect where her foot stepped a moment away
as if to run. I could see in the dust the curve of her arch,
the five toes spread, the track looking like something wanted to escape,
some animal that had tried to leap away from what pursued her,
her father-in-law, her husband, the room. Dust withered
around her, then a whimper she must have heard
from a bed, a child, I think now a son, troubled by the night
and the voice of his grandfather, a sound he didn't know,
not well, not yet, and, in the end, not at all. The trail my father left,
the wet prints leading in from the door, the swirls of burnt
sawdust he brought in with the snow, and the ones he took
leading out, his trail obscured, an arrival and departure,
his glass on the wooden crate by the chair, a faint circle there
when I picked it up, and the smear inside
where his tongue had licked it clean. And the trail
I didn't make, the one I waited for, the marks my feet had left
coming into the room of my father, and the other trail,
the one I would make in what was then almost a moment and wasn't,
the door left open a crack, snow and dust withering
across the floor, so that I thought if I got down on my knees
and put my head to the worn wood, the dust would whisper me a song,
one I could learn about the night outside where the moon was
on the ice road shining, the music playing as loud as it could my heart.

WHAT LANGUAGE CAN'T REACH

And the only way I know how to do that is to stand far off
as if on a low hill under a moon
watching a passenger train stopped
at a siding in the distance of a prairie night in winter.
In the snow and watching. That far away. That sure.

Books by Patrick Lane

Poetry

Letters from the Savage Mind, (Very Stone House, Vancouver, BC: 1966)

Separations (New Books, Trumansburg, NY: 1969)

Mountain Oysters (Very Stone House in Transit, Vernon, BC: 1970)

On the Street (Very Stone House in Transit, Vernon, BC: 1970)

Hiway 401 Rhapsody (Very Stone House in Transit, Vernon, BC: 1971)

The Sun Has Begun to Eat the Mountain (Ingluvin, Montreal, PQ: 1972)

Passing Into Storm (Traumerei, Vernon, BC: 1973)

Beware the Months of Fire (Anansi, Toronto, ON: 1974)

Unborn Things: South American Poems (Harbour, Madeira Park, BC: 1975)

Albino Pheasants (Harbour, Madeira Park, BC, 1977)

Poems: New & Selected (Oxford, Toronto, ON: 1978)

No Longer Two People (with Lorna Crozier), (Turnstone, Winnipeg, MB: 1979)

The Measure (Black Moss, Windsor, ON: 1980)

Old Mother (Oxford, Toronto, ON: 1982)

Woman in the Dust (Mosaic, Toronto, ON: 1983)

A Linen Crow, A Caftan Magpie (Thistledown, Saskatoon, SK: 1985)

Selected Poems (Oxford, Toronto, ON: 1987)

Winter (Coteau, Regina, SK: 1990)

Mortal Remains (Exile, Toronto, ON: 1991)

Too Spare, Too Fierce (Harbour, Madeira Park, BC: 1995)

Selected Poems 1977–1997 (Harbour, Madeira Park, BC: 1997)

The Bare Plum of Winter Rain (Harbour, Madeira Park, BC: 2000)

Go Leaving Strange (Harbour, Madeira Park, BC: 2004)

Syllable of Stone (Arc Publications, Todmorden, Lancashire, UK: 2005)

Last Water Song (Harbour, Madeira Park, BC: 2007)

Children's

Milford & Me (Coteau Books, Regina, SK: 1989)

Fiction

How Do You Spell Beautiful (Fifth House, Saskatoon, SK: 1992)

Red Dog Red Dog (McClelland & Stewart, Toronto, ON: 2008)

Non-fiction

There Is a Season: A Memoir in a Garden (McClelland & Stewart, Toronto, ON: 2004)

Anthologies (Editor with Lorna Crozier)

Breathing Fire (Harbour, Madeira Park, BC: 1994)

Addicted: Notes From the Belly of the Beast (Greystone, Vancouver, BC: 2001)

Breathing Fire 2 (Nightwood, Gibsons, BC: 2004)

Index of Titles